Join in –
Jump on!

Scripture Union
207-209 Queensway, Bletchley, Milton Keynes, MK2 2EB, UK

Writers: Lesley Blight, Jenny Davies, Sue Dunn, Marjory Francis, Muriel Griffith, Beth McLean, Elspeth Macleod
Editor: Marjory Francis
Design: Chris Gander Design Associates Illustration: Branwen Thomas

ISBN 185999 3214
Reprinted 2001
Printed and bound in the UK by Ebenezer Baylis & Son Ltd, The Trinity Press, Worcester and
London

To help you

Did you know the Bible is made up of lots of books?
You will be reading from these books in **Join in – Jump on!**
Exodus 1 Samuel 2 Samuel Psalms
See if you can find them in the Old Testament books below and colour
them in.

Genesis Exodus Leviticus Numbers Deuteronomy Joshua Judges Ruth 1 Samuel 2 Samuel 1 Kings 2 Kings 1 Chronicles 2 Chronicles Ezra Nehemiah Esther Job Psalms Proverbs Ecclesiastes Song of Songs Isaiah Jeremiah Lamentations Ezekiel Daniel Hosea Joel Amos Obadiah Jonah Micah Nahum Habakkuk Zephaniah Haggai Zechariah Malachi

Now see if you can find and colour the ones you will be reading from the
New Testament:
Matthew Mark Luke Acts 2 Timothy

Matthew Mark Luke John Acts Romans 1 Corinthians 2 Corinthians Galatians Ephesians Philippians Colossians 1 Thessalonians 2 Thessalonians 1 Timothy 2 Timothy Titus Philemon Hebrews James 1 Peter 2 Peter 1 John 2 John 3 John Jude Revelation

In this book find out about:

Jesus calls Matthew *Days 1 to 3*
Hidden treasure *Days 4 to 5*
A farmer in a field *Days 6 to 8*
Big sister Miriam *Days 9 to 11*
God calls Moses *Days 12 to 14*
Moses the leader *Days 15 to 19*
Jesus heals people *Days 20 to 25*
A challenge for David *Days 26 to 30*
David the king *Days 31 to 34*
Jesus and the children *Days 35 to 39*
I want to praise God *Days 40 to 44*
People of the new church *Days 45 to 50*

Plus:
Lots of Extra pages
All over the world!
The joke and puzzle page!

How to use this book

There are Bible activities in this book to keep you busy for 50 days. You will find stories about people in the Bible and lots of ideas to help you get to know God better. Each day you will find

- something to read
- a puzzle or questions to answer
- something to look up in the Bible
- a prayer idea

Sometimes there are Extra fun ideas too!

Here are some ideas for using **Join in – Jump on!**

- It's best to read it every day if you can, but it doesn't matter if you miss days sometimes. Just carry on from where you got up to.
- It's OK to use **Join in – Jump on!** on your own, or you might like someone to help you.
- Most days you will just need a Bible and a pencil to use with **Join in – Jump on!**
- It's best to save the Extra pages for when you have lots of time. You will need to collect other things to use for these.
- Try to find somewhere quiet to read your Bible and **Join in – Jump on!**

So make sure you have a Bible and a pencil, and jump on to **Join in – Jump on!** now!

Jesus calls Matthew

Matthew sat at his table by the roadside. His job was to collect the tax money for the Romans. People would come and pay him, but they didn't like doing it because the Romans were their enemies.

One day a crowd came past. He knew they wouldn't look *his* way. But then one of them did! It was the teacher, Jesus! "Come with me," he said. Matthew didn't need to be asked twice. He left his table and all the money, and went off with Jesus.

LOOk up Matthew chapter 9, verse 9 to find this story.

a ayer

Jesus was with a big crowd of people, but he still noticed Matthew. Can you find Jesus and Matthew in this crowd?

Thank you, esus, that you always notice me, even when I'm in a crowd.

Jesus calls Matthew

Matthew was so pleased to have Jesus as his friend that he asked him to dinner at his house. He asked lots of his other friends too, because he wanted them to meet Jesus.

LOOk up

this story in **Luke chapter 5, verse 29**. (Matthew is called by his other name of Levi here.)

If you were inviting Jesus and your other friends to a party at your house, what delicious food would you give them?
Draw it here:

prayer time

Write the names of some of your friends in this prayer:

Dear God, thank you for my friends

_____ and

_____ . Help me to be a good friend to them. Thank you that Jesus wants to be our very best friend.

Jesus calls Matthew

Some people thought Matthew's friends were too bad for Jesus. Some of them were tax collectors like Matthew and some had done other wrong things. But Jesus didn't mind meeting them. He wanted to be friends with everyone and help them to start living good lives.

Read about it in **Luke chapter 5, verses 30 to 31.** (Remember Matthew is called Levi here.)

Jesus said that when we need something we go to the person who can help us. Match the people here:

a prayer

Thank you, Jesus, that when I say sorry for the wrong things I have done, you will forgive me.

When we need to be forgiven we can go to Jesus.

Hidden treasure

Matthew wrote down some of Jesus' stories for us to read. This is one of them:

A man was digging in a field. Suddenly his spade struck something. What was it? It was treasure, buried long ago! The man knew it would be wrong to just take it. So he covered it up again and went to see if he had enough money to buy the field. He had to sell everything he had, but he knew it was worth it. Soon the field and the treasure belonged to him!

Read this story in **Matthew chapter 13, verse 44.**

The man found hidden treasure. See if you can find the words hidden here.
(Colour in every x and z)

x	z	J	z	e	s	x	x	u	z
s	z	t	x	z	o	z	z	l	z
d	x	a	z	z	s	x	t	x	x
o	z	r	z	x	y	z	a	x	b
z	x	o	z	u	x	z	t	x	t
x	r	z	e	x	x	a	z	x	s
z	u	x	r	z	e	z	x		

a prayer

Lord Jesus, thank you for the stories we find in the Bible.

Hidden treasure

Another story Jesus told was about a man who was looking for jewels.

LOOk up Matthew chapter 13, verse 45 to

see what sort of jewels they were:

When he found a specially fine one, what did he sell so that he could buy it? Look in **verse 46** to find out.

Jewels are very special and have beautiful colours. What colours would these jewels be?

ruby

emerald

amethyst

sapphire

prayer time

Everything **about Jesus is special. Say a prayer thanking Jesus for how special he is.**

A treasure box to make

1 Cut a strip of wrapping paper a little bit wider than the box, to go right round the sides. Glue it down carefully, and fold and glue the extra paper over the top edge.

2 Cut another piece large enough to cover the lid and fold over the edges. Glue this on. Ask an adult to help you to make the corners neat.

3 Cut strips of gold paper. Glue them across the top and around the sides of the box. Make a gold padlock to fix at the front.

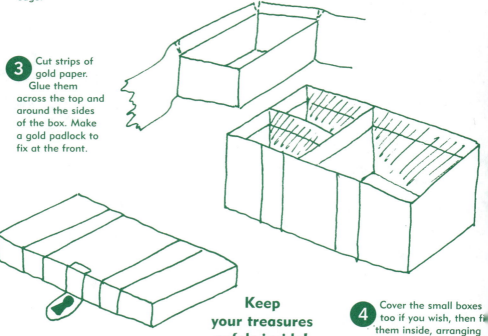

Keep your treasures safely inside!

4 Cover the small boxes too if you wish, then fi them inside, arranging them carefully before you fix them down.

A farmer in a field

Matthew wrote about Jesus telling a story. So many people wanted to listen that Jesus had to sit somewhere very unusual.

 Read Matthew **chapter 13, verses 1 and 2** to see where it was. Draw it in the picture.

Look at **verse 3** to see what the story was about.

The story was about a

☐ ☐ ☐ ☐ ☐ ☐

a   m   f   r   r   e

Read some more of the story next time!

Prayer time

Thank Jesus that we can enjoy the stories he told too.

A farmer in a field

Jesus was telling a story about a farmer. The busy man threw seeds all over his field. Where did they land?

Read the next part of the story in **Matthew chapter 13, verses 4 to 7** to find out.

Some seeds fell along the road and were eaten by

_ _ _ _ _

Some seeds fell where there were

_ _ _ _ _

Some seeds fell where there were

_ _ _ _ _

Did any of these seeds grow? Tick the right answer.

YES   NO

a prayer

Jesus said that the seeds that fell in these places were like people who listened to what he said, but didn't take notice for very long.

Help me, Jesus, to listen and take notice of what you say.

A farmer in a field

On Day 7 we heard that some of the seeds in Jesus' story didn't grow. What do you think happened to the others?

2 30 3

5 100

14 60 50

Matthew chapter 13, verse 8 to find out. How many new seeds did some plants grow? Colour in the right numbers.

Draw lots of new seeds on these plants.

prayer time

The seeds that fell on the good ground grew. Jesus said these were like people who listened carefully to him and did what he said.

Think about the people who tell you about Jesus and say thank you to God for them.

Extra!

A seed pattern

Sort the seeds out into different shapes, sizes and colours on the saucers. (**Never eat seeds or dried beans** unless a grown up says you may. Some are poisonous unless they are cooked.) Draw a wiggly line on the paper plate to make different sections. Glue a section at a time and sprinkle one sort of seed on it. Fill in the sections with the different seeds until the plate is covered. Leave the plate flat to dry. Tip off the spare seeds.

Make a loop of wool or ribbon and fix to the back. Hang up your plate.

Grow a plant

Plant different seeds in each pot. Write what they are on the label. Water them carefully and look each day to see if they are growing. Some may take a long time!

Lemon

Big sister Miriam

I'm Miriam. I was born and brought up in Egypt. Long ago my people, the Hebrews, came from Israel to Egypt. The king made them welcome but the new king doesn't like us and makes us work very hard as his slaves. He says there are too many of us and now he's trying to kill all baby boys. My mummy had a baby boy three months ago. He's too big now to hide at home, so we had to think of another idea. I'm hiding amongst the tall grass at the river's edge to see what will happen.

Why is Miriam by the river?

Read Exodus chapter 2, verses 1 to 4 to find out.

a **rayer**

10
9
8
1 · · 12   · 11   · 7
2
3   · 4   · 5   · 6

ear God, please show me how I can be a helper in my family.

What was Miriam's baby brother hidden in? Join the numbers to see.

Big sister Miriam

It's Miriam here, hiding by the river. I can see the king's daughter coming along. She's noticed the basket and I can hear her asking her servant to bring it to her. I hope she will be kind to my baby brother. The princess is opening the basket. Baby is crying. What will she do with him?

Find out what the princess thinks by reading **Exodus chapter 2, verses 5 and 6**.

Help the princess find the baby in the basket.

a prayer

Thank you, God, that you always care for me.

Big sister Miriam

The princess found my baby brother. That gave me a good idea. I came out of hiding and spoke to the princess. "Do you want me to find a Hebrew woman to take care of the baby for you?" "Yes, please," she said. I ran as fast as I could and brought our own mummy. The princess asked mummy to take care of our baby and even said she will pay her. When he is older we must take him to the palace to live there. It is lovely to look after baby and not be frightened.

Read the story in **Exodus chapter 2, verses 7 to 10**.

The princess gave my baby brother a new name. What was it? Put the letters in the right spaces.

a prayer

Thank you, God, for all the people who look after me.

A basket card

Trace the shape below to make a basket card.

Or

Make a *Plasticine* model of the story.

Roll some *Plasticine* into a long snake. Make part of it into an oval shape and then build up the sides of the basket by going round and round the sides. Make a baby from *Plasticine* and put it in the basket. You could make the river and tall grass from blue and green paper.

God calls Moses

I'm Moses. I stayed in the palace until I was grown up, but then I did something bad, so I ran away. I stayed in the land of Midian at Jethro's home and married his daughter. It was my job to look after Jethro's sheep and goats. One day, I took the animals to God's special mountain, Sinai. There I saw something very strange!

Read Exodus chapter 3, verses 1 to 4 to find out what it was.

a prayer

ank you, God, that ou know me by my name

Join the dots to see what Moses saw.
Draw the flames.

God spoke to Moses by his name.

Day 13

God calls Moses

God spoke to me, Moses, at the burning bush. He said, "My people the Hebrews are being cruelly treated by the Egyptians." Then he said I had to do something to help. What was it?

Find out by reading **Exodus 3, verses 9 and 10**.

E   p   y

God told Moses to go back to

t   g

Find the letters to make the word.

a prayer

Thank you, God, th you spoke in a special way to Moses. Thank you, God, that you speak to me too.

God calls Moses

When God asked me, Moses, to go back to Egypt and speak to the king, I felt it was far too hard for me to do. God promised to be with me, and that one day I would come back with all my own people to this

_ _ _ _ _ _ _ _

Find out from **Exodus chapter 3, verse 12**. What did God promise?

Fill in the words on the stepping stones.

will

I

you

with

be

prayer time

Think of hard things you have to do and pray this prayer:
Dear God, please help me when I have hard things to do.

Moses the leader

Moses wasn't sure that he was the right person to lead the people for God.

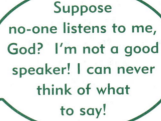

Suppose no-one listens to me, God? I'm not a good speaker! I can never think of what to say!

"I will give you the words to say," promised God.

Moses begged "Please send someone else."

"You are the one I want to do this job, Moses," said God, "but I will let your brother Aaron go with you. He is a good speaker and will help you, I promise!"

LOOk up Exodus chapter 5, verses 1 and 2 to find out what happened when Moses and Aaron went to the king of Egypt.

a prayer

But Moses and Aaron didn't give up. They kept going back to the king. Colour all the shapes with dots to find out how many times the king said "No".

Dear God, please help me not to give up when things are hard.

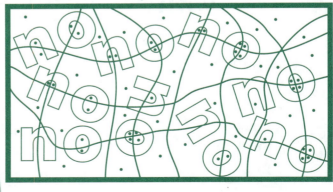

Moses the leader

God knew the king would change his mind. Something was going to happen! "Choose your best animal to have for a special meal tonight," Moses told the people. "Put some of the blood from the animal on the doorposts of your houses. It will show that you are God's special people. Then get ready for a long journey!"
Just as God had promised, the king did change his mind.

Read what he said in **Exodus chapter 12, verses 31 and 32**.

After that God's people had a special party every year. It reminded them that God heard their prayers and kept his promises. Write the first letter of each object to find out the name of the party.

Thank you, God, that you hear my prayers and always keep your promises.

Moses the leader

The people left Egypt and set off to find the country God had promised to give them. They probably felt a bit scared.
What would it be like?
Would they get lost?
Would there be danger?
Who would help them?
God knew how they were feeling! Read **Exodus chapter 13, verses 21 and 22** to find out what he did.

Write **night** and **day** below the correct picture.

prayer time

Are there times when you feel a bit scared? Talk to God about it just now. Did you know that he says "I am with you always" (Matthew chapter 28, verse 20)?

Moses the leader

Moses and the people are running away from Egypt.
But now they seem to be trapped! What were they
to do? In front of them was the Red Sea, and
behind them, the Egyptian army was catching up
fast! The king wasn't going to let them go after all!
What do you think happened?

Read about it in **Exodus chapter 14, verses 21 and 22**.

a **rayer**

Thank you, God,
that you are so
great. Please help
me to remember
hat nothing is too
hard for you.

The people were safe! God is
so great he can control the
wind and the sea. Draw
Moses and the people walking
between the walls of water.

Moses the leader

Do you remember who Miriam was? (Look back to day 10 to see if you are right.) Miriam had escaped from Egypt with Moses, and now she was safe too! When Miriam remembered all the ways that God had looked after them, she felt so happy she wanted to

s ☐ ☐ ☐

and **d** ☐ ☐ ☐ ☐

Read Exodus chapter 15, verses 20 and 21 to find out what she did!

prayer time

Do you have a favourite song about God? Why not sing it now?
Or you could sing this one to the tune of *Frère Jacques*.

> God is great! God is great!
> Praise him! Praise him!
> He looked after Moses, he looked after Moses,
> God is great! God is great!
>
> God is great! God is great!
> Praise him! Praise him!
> He looks after me, he looks after me,
> God is great! God is great!

Make up a prayer thanking God for all the ways he looks after you.

Jesus heals people

One day an army captain came to see Jesus. He was very worried and asked Jesus for help.

> My servant is at home. He is in such pain that he can't even move!

LOOk up

Matthew chapter 8, verses 5 to 7 to find out what Jesus said.

Fill in the gaps with **a, e, i, o,** or **u** to complete Jesus' reply.

I will

g   nd

h   l

h m

a prayer

Jesus was never too busy to listen to the people who came to him. He always helped those in need.

Do you know anyone who needs Jesus' help? Use this prayer to pray for him or her:
Thank you, Jesus, that you are never too busy to listen to us and to help us. Please help

Jesus heals people

The army captain didn't want Jesus to come back to his house. "I am not good enough for you to come to my house," he said. He had another idea.

> I am used to giving orders. My soldiers always do what I tell them. Just give the order and I know my servant will get better.

You can read this story in **Matthew chapter 8, verses 8 and 9**.

a prayer

Thank you, Jesus, that you are so powerful.

Draw somebody here who tells people what to do.	Draw somebody here who must obey them.

The army captain knew how powerful Jesus was. He knew that Jesus could make his servant better.

Jesus heals people

Jesus was amazed that the army captain trusted him to heal his servant without seeing him. He told the army captain, "You can go home now. Because you knew I could help you, your servant will be healed."

LOOk up

Matthew chapter 8, verse 13 to find out what happened next.

Draw a ring round the correct words in each line to make the last sentence in the story:

Three days later   At once   Next year

Jesus   the servant   the army captain

got worse   died   was healed

a prayer

How do you think the army captain felt when he got home and saw that his servant was well again? Draw his face.

Think of times when you need Jesus to help you.

Dear Jesus, help me to trust that you can help me, especially when

Jesus heals people

Many people came to see Jesus at the house where he was staying. Four men brought a man who could not walk. He had to lie on a mat all day. Can you draw him on his mat?

(If you have time, read **Mark chapter 2, verses 1 to 4** to find out how the men got their friend into the house.)

Jesus told the man not to worry. Then he said a very surprising thing.

LOOk up Matthew chapter 9, verse 2 to

find out what Jesus said. Check your answer by colouring in every b and d in the line below. The letters left over will tell you what Jesus said.

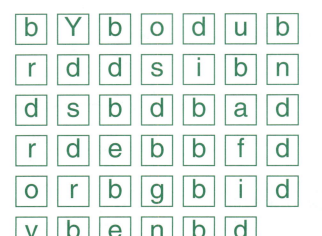

b	Y	b	o	d	u	b
r	d	d	s	i	b	n
d	s	b	d	b	a	d
r	d	e	b	b	f	d
o	r	b	g	b	i	d
v	b	e	n	b	d	

Jesus knew that it is important for us to be forgiven for the wrong things we do.

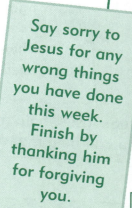

prayer time

Say sorry to Jesus for any wrong things you have done this week. Finish by thanking him for forgiving you.

Jesus heals people

Jesus had forgiven the man for the wrong things he had done. Now he wanted to help the man get well. Remember that the man could not walk. What Jesus told him to do must have seemed very strange!

Matthew chapter 9, verses 5 and 6 to find out what Jesus said. He told the man to do three things. Number them in the correct order.

○ **Pick up your mat.**

○ **Get up.**

○ **Go home.**

In the space draw the man doing what Jesus told him to.

Thank you, Jesus, that you care about our bodies. Please look after people who cannot move easily.

Jesus had healed the man's body. All the people were amazed and praised God. I expect the man praised God too, don't you? Jesus had put him right on the inside and on the outside.

Jesus heals people

Jesus didn't just heal the army captain's servant and the man who couldn't walk. Everywhere he went he taught the people about God. Often sick people would be brought to him. He cared about each one and made them all well again.

 **Matthew chapter 9, verse 35.**

True or False? Did you read the verse carefully? Read the sentences below and tick ✓ the ones which are true. Cross out ~~like this~~ the ones which are wrong.

- Jesus went into every town and village.
- He went into the supermarkets.
- He went into the places where the people met.
- He taught the people how to do sums.
- He told the people the good news about God's kingdom.
- He healed sick people.
- He took the sick people to hospital.

a prayer

Thank you, Jesus, that you care about everyone, whoever they are. Thank you that you care about me.

Extra!

Many people brought their friends and family to Jesus. You too can bring your friends and family to Jesus by praying for them. Why not make a prayer chain to help you remember?

1 Take a long strip of paper and fold it six times to make seven sections.

2 On the top section draw the shape of a person, making sure that the hands and feet touch the edge.

3 Cut through all the layers to make a chain of people. (Don't cut the folds or the people will not be joined together!)

4 On each person write a day of the week and someone you would like to pray for.

5 Hang up your prayer chain near your bed. When you get up or when you go to bed, pray for that day's person.

A challenge for David

Fierce enemies were attacking. King Saul called for brave young men to join his army. The soldiers lined up for battle. Then the biggest man they had ever seen strutted out of the enemy camp. He shouted at them.

Read about it in **1 Samuel chapter 17, verses 2 to 11**.

Fill in the words:

The giant was named **G** _ _ _ _ _ _ (verse 4).

He challenged anyone to **f**_ _ **h** _ (verse 8).

He was dressed in bronze **a** _ **m** _ _ _ (verse 5).

and carried a heavy **s** _ _ _ **r** (verse 7).

His enormous **s** _ _ _ **l** _ (verse 7).

was carried by a **s** _ _ **d** _ _ _ (verse 7).

a prayer

G						

What word have you made in the dark box?

When Goliath's voice roared across the valley, the soldiers shook in their sandals. They had forgotten that God was always with them.

Are there things that frighten you? Talk to God about them.

Father God, when I am afraid, especially of _____ help me to remember that you are always with me.

A challenge for David

Some of my big brothers have gone to join King Saul's army to fight those fierce enemies. I'm just 'little David', too young to go, worse luck!
I was left at home to help Dad on the farm. Most days I look after the sheep. Today I'm going…

Read

Read about it in **1 Samuel chapter 17, verses 17 to 26**.

David did what his father told him to do whether it was fun or boring.

Will you help to set the table please?

I want to watch TV.

I will help.

It can wait until tomorrow.

Please tidy your room.

I'm coming!

The hamster needs cleaning out.

I can't be bothered.

a prayer

Would you like me to do it?

Join up answers that would please God.

Father God, please help me to be helpful when I am asked.

Have you done as you were asked today?

A challenge for David

David reached the army camp and started to look for his brothers. He saw Goliath and heard him shouting. He asked the soldiers why everyone was afraid of him.

David said "I'll go and fight him."

Look in **1 Samuel chapter 17, verses 36 and 37** to find out why David thought he could beat Goliath.

1 Samuel chapter 17, verses 38 to 40 to see how David got ready for his fight.

It was great to wear real soldier's kit, but David was sensible and he knew it was too big and grown-up for him.

Join the dots. Which one is best for a child to wear? ✓

a prayer

Dear God, David didn't wait to be useful until he was a man. Please make me useful now.

A challenge for David

Goliath

David

Goliath and David chose their weapons and walked towards each other. Join the weapons to the right person.

Read But David had a secret as well.

what he said in **1 Samuel chapter 17, verse 47** and fill in the word.

David's secret was that the **L _ _ _** was going to help him.

Are there hard things you will have to do this week?

prayer time

Thank you, God, that I can always trust you to help me when things are hard for me.

A challenge for David

Who won?

You will find the end of the story in **1 Samuel chapter 17, verses 48 to 50**.

- Everyone saw that little David, using simple weapons, had killed giant Goliath.
- Everyone knew that David won because he trusted God to help him.
- Everyone understood how great God is!

What an exciting true story!

Ask a grown-up to read you the whole of **chapter 17**.

Can you number the drawings in the right order?

David slings a stone.

Everyone is afraid of Goliath.

Goliath is dead.

David talks to King Saul.

a prayer

Thank you, God, f⟨
all the exciting stori⟨
you have given us i⟨
the Bible.

Extra!

Measure up!

Goliath was nearly 3 metres tall.
How would he manage in your house?
You will need a ruler or a tape measure.

Could he get in the door?

The door is ⬚ high.

Could he lie down in the bath?

The bath is ⬚ long.

Would he fit in your bed?

My bed is ⬚ long.

I am ⬚ tall.

David the king

God told Samuel, "Go to Bethlehem and find Jesse. I have chosen one of his sons to be the next king. I will show you which one."

There was excitement when Samuel arrived! Everyone joined him to worship God.

Jesse came in with his seven fine grown-up sons. Samuel looked at the eldest and thought, "Here he is!" But God said, "No." Samuel looked at his brother, tall and handsome. But God said, "No."

You can read the rest of the story in **1 Samuel chapter 16, verses 10 to 12**.

David was young and unimportant so he was left out. But God knew that inside he was just the sort of person he needed.

How many differences can you see between these two men?

a prayer

Father God, you know all about me. Help me to be the sort of person you can trust and choose to serve you.

David the king

It was many years since Samuel had told David that God had chosen him to be king. David was a man now, and Saul was still king. He was jealous of David and kept trying to kill him. Sometimes Saul took his whole army to hunt him. But one dark night David found Saul's camp.

You can read about it in **1 Samuel chapter 26, verse 7**.

Saul asleep! David could get rid of him! But read **verses 9 and 11** to find out what David said.

Cross out the wrong answer

Sh! Sh! David, shall I kill him?

Yes   No

God helped David to do what was right. He knew God would help him to become king one day.

Come out and play with us!

Play in the garden, James.

a rayer

When it is easy to do wrong, help me, God, to say NO.

If James did right, what would he say to the girls?

Yes   No

David the king

God had promised – "I've chosen you to be king."
David trusted… David prayed… and David waited.
At last God made David king.
Join the dots to crown King David.

You can read about it in **2 Samuel chapter 5, verses 1 to 4.**
Was David 12 15 21 25 or 30 years old when he became king?

12

15

21

25

30

a
prayer

David had to wait a long, long time, but he trusted God to keep his promise.
See if you can read what David wrote.
(Look at the words in a mirror.)

Thank you, God, that I know you will keep your promises. Help me to keep mine.

He will never forget his promises, not in thousands of years.
Psalm 105:8

David the king

God had promised "I will give you good things."
Fill in the word:

o d G

David trusted _ _ _.

d G o

David thanked _ _ _ and David praised
him too.

God promised that he would make David a great
king and show his love and kindness to him and his
family.

When David heard this he thanked and praised God.
You can read his prayer in
2 Samuel chapter 7, verses 28 and 29.

Be like David and pray for your
family.

Draw a picture of your family or
those who look after you here:

a prayer

Great and
wonderful
God, thank
you for my
family. Please
take care of
us today and
always.

All over the world!

In this book you are finding out about God and his Son Jesus.

Did you know that boys and girls all over the world hear and read stories about Jesus too? Write in the places where you think these children are learning about him.

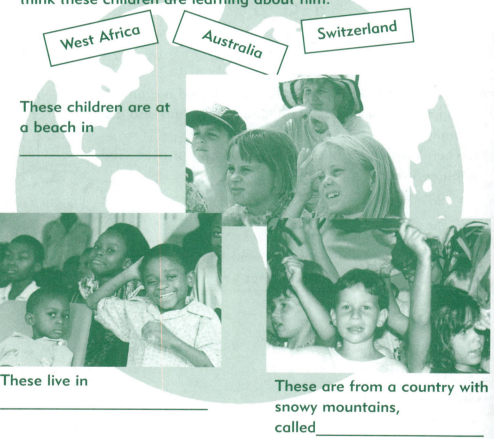

West Africa

Australia

Switzerland

These children are at a beach in

_____

These live in

_____

These are from a country with snowy mountains, called_____

Is there someone from your church who works in another country? Perhaps you could find out from them about some girls and boys there who love Jesus. You might even like to write to one of them!

Jesus and the children

Some people wanted their children to meet Jesus. You can read what happened in **Matthew chapter 19 verses 13 to 15.**

The disciples, who were friends of Jesus, did not think it was a good idea , and got cross about it.

Solve the code to find what Jesus said:

c	d	e	h	i	l	m	n	o	r	t
✳	▲	▼	★	✖	❖	✚	☀	✤	♣	☆

a prayer

Jesus made it clear that he wanted to meet the children. If you had been there, how do you think you would have felt? Happy? Scared? Special? Surprised?

Thank you, Jesus, that you had time for children. Thank you that you always have time for me.

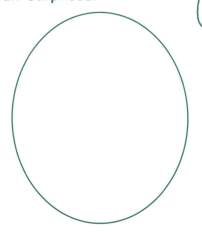

Draw your face to show it!

Jesus and the children

Who do you think is the most important person:

in your house? in your school?
Draw them and write
their names.

Jesus' friends wanted to know who Jesus thought was important.

Read **Matthew chapter 18, verses 1 and 2** to find out what he did. Often people didn't really notice children. Jesus wanted his friends to know that children mattered to him and that he thought adults could sometimes learn things from children.

a prayer

Colour one word to say what Jesus thinks about children:
Jesus thinks that children are

naughty
important
nasty

Lord Jesus, than you that you think children matter – and that means me! Help me to remember that you think I'm special.

Jesus and the children

In today's story everyone seemed excited to see Jesus. Read it in **Matthew chapter 21, verses 7 to 10**.

Find the right words to fill the gaps and tell the story. Choose from this list:

donkey   Jerusalem   crowds   trees   shouted

Jesus and his friends were going to **1**. Jesus rode on a **2**. The **3** put clothes and branches from **5** on the path. They **4** "Hooray! Praise God!".

Whose name have you found?

If you had been in the crowd what would you have done? Draw yourself here:

prayer time

Can you think of something about Jesus that makes you want to cheer? Tell him what it is!

Not everyone was happy. Read about it in **verses 15 and 16**. Some people complained but Jesus was glad that the children were cheering him.

Jesus and the children

See how many differences you can find between the two pictures:

A man came to see Jesus even though his daughter had died. He must have been sad, but he didn't give up hope. He asked Jesus for help.

Read about it in **Matthew chapter 9, verses 18 and 19**.

Are you surprised that Jesus went with the man?   Yes ☐   No ☐

Can you say why?

The man must have known something about Jesus. Tick the ones you think he might have said.

a prayer

Thank you, Jesus, that you wanted to help. Help me to remember that you're always there for me.

☐ Jesus can help.

☐ Jesus will care about my daughter.

☐ Jesus won't have time for my child.

✓ Jesus will be too busy.

Jesus and the children

Jesus wants children to know that he is their friend. But he isn't just an ordinary friend. He is God's Son, so he is a perfect friend. He can do wonderful things. In today's story he did something amazing! You can read it in **Matthew chapter 9, verses 23 to 25**.

Everyone was upset because the girl was dead. They must have wondered what Jesus was going to do. Imagine how they must have felt when he told her to get up – and she did!

Draw a picture of the end of the story here.

a prayer

Thank you, Jesus, that you are so amazing, so special, and that you want to be my friend!

Extra!

All about me!

Play this game with a friend or member of your family. You will need a counter for each player and a die.

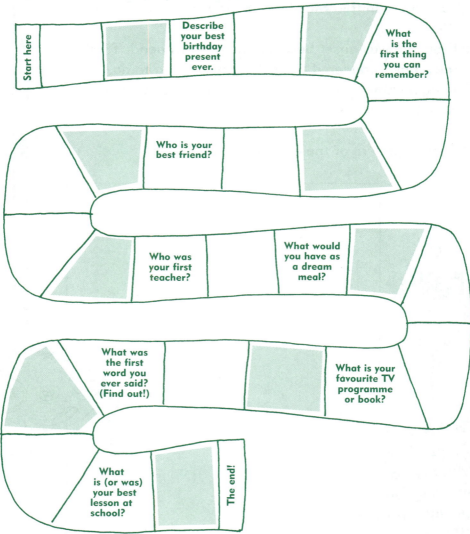

Start here

Describe your best birthday present ever.

What is the first thing you can remember?

Who is your best friend?

Who was your first teacher?

What would you have as a dream meal?

What was the first word you ever said? (Find out!)

What is your favourite TV programme or book?

The end!

What is (or was) your best lesson at school?

Jesus knows all about you – and loves you whether you're young or old!

I want to praise God

Can you think of a time when you've done something well and you have been praised for it? It probably made you feel good to know people were happy. Have you ever praised someone else for doing something you liked?

King David and his people knew how great God was! They had seen him do amazing things. They wanted to show him that they thought he was wonderful.

Read 2 Samuel chapter 6, verse 5.

a prayer

Put the letters in the right boxes to say what they did.

e l a d p y

They ⬜⬜⬜⬜⬜ music and ⬜⬜⬜⬜⬜⬜ and ⬜⬜⬜⬜.

e n a c d   s g n a

Finish the sentences and use them to talk to God.

I want to praise you, God, because you always ⬜⬜⬜⬜⬜⬜⬜⬜⬜ I want to praise you, God, because you never ⬜⬜⬜⬜⬜⬜⬜⬜⬜ I want to say a special thank you, God, because

⬜⬜⬜⬜⬜⬜⬜⬜⬜⬜⬜⬜⬜

I want to praise God

Can you find the names of these musical instruments in the word search? They may go across or down the square!

s	l	o	d	n	x	g
r	h	a	r	p	j	u
b	n	e	u	z	w	i
t	r	u	m	p	e	t
a	s	b	x	i	g	a
f	z	l	n	a	o	r
q	y	v	m	n	d	l
e	j	n	s	o	p	h

drum

piano

guitar

trumpet

harp

King David was good at playing one of these. Read **Psalm 144, verse 9** and find out which one. David sometimes played it to make other people feel happy. In today's reading he is playing and singing a new song to God. He wants to tell God how great he thinks God is.

See if you can make up a new song to sing to God, perhaps to a well-known tune.

Think of something you can do well. Maybe it's drawing pictures, or helping at home, or being someone's friend. Say thank you to God that you can do it!

I want to praise God

King David knew that God had always been with him. God had told him he would be king and it had happened! God had looked after him and kept him safe. He knew he could trust God and he could look back and see that things had worked out well.

Read how David talks to God about it and says thank you to him in **Psalm 21, verses 3 to 5**.

Can you think of some good times that you have had? Fill in the gaps for the ones you've enjoyed and draw the best one ever!

a day out to _____

a holiday in _____

my _____ th birthday

Prayer time

I enjoyed this most!

Not everything is great fun. Sometimes things don't make us happy. But God promises to be with us through the good and the not-so-good times. Make up your own prayer to say thank you to him for always being there.

Day 43

I want to praise God

When things weren't going well for King David, he would talk to God about it. Sometimes he would be sad or worried and he would tell God how he was feeling. But then he would remember something that helped him.

Read **Psalm 13, verses 5 and 6** and write the first letter of each picture to see what he remembered.

Can you think of ways that God has been good to you? Maybe there are things here that he has given you. Follow the chain and write down the letters as they come to find four.

1 _ _ _   3 _ _ _ _

2 _ _ _ _ _ _   4 _ _ _ _ _ _

Fill in the gaps and then say this prayer to God.

Today I feel _____ because _____.
I am glad that you are there and I know you understand and care!

I want to praise God

Sometimes David wanted to praise God not for what God did, nor for what God gave him, nor because God had looked after him – but just because of what God is like.

Shade in these squares to find what David knew about God.

A1,A5,A13 B1,B13 C1,C3,C5,C7,C8, C9,C11,C12,C13
D1,D2,D5,D7,D9,D11,D13 E1,E3,E5, E7,E9,E11,E12,E13,

	1	2	3	4	5	6	7	8	9	10	11	12	13
A													
B													
C													
D													
E													

He knew God was _ _ _ _ . Read what David said in **Psalm 103, verses 1 and 2**.

David also knew that God is holy (that means completely good.) Only God can be that!

Cross out x,y and z to find more words to describe what God is like.

xpxerxfexctx   yloyvinygy   zgzrezatz

[   ]   [   ]   [   ]

a rayer

Use one of the words (or one of your own) to talk to God like David did.

"Dear God, I want to praise you. Help me never to forget how [   ] you are!"

Extra!

Make a praise mobile!

Trace the shape onto a piece of paper or thin card. Cut it out along the outside lines. Fold along the dotted lines. In each triangle, colour something for which you would like to say thank you to God. Fold together and put some glue on the shaded areas to fix your shape. Make a loop and hang your shape up. Make lots of shapes saying great things about God!

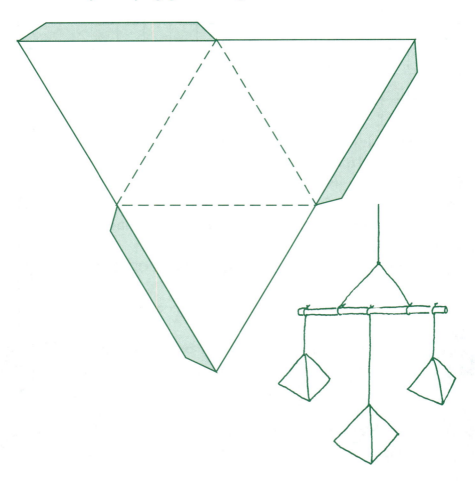

People of the new church

Today we are thinking about Jesus' friends after he had gone back to heaven. They met together and thanked God for Jesus and for his Holy Spirit. They helped each other by sharing and also gave things to the poor. Dorcas helped too. One day everyone was very sad because Dorcas died. Her friends in Joppa sent two men to fetch Peter.

Read this part of the story in **Acts chapter 9, verses 36 to 39**. What was Dorcas specially good at?

i   s   n   e   g   w

Dorcas used her ☐☐☐☐☐☐ to help others.

prayer time

Tick the things you are good at. Circle the ones you could use to help or please others.

drawing

painting

music

running

looking after animals

Help me, dear God, to use the things I can do to help or please others.

making things

People of the new church

When Peter heard the news about Dorcas he hurried to Joppa. The people were sad because their friend Dorcas was dead, but Peter went into the room and told her to sit up. Dorcas sat up straightaway. All the people in the town were amazed at what God had done. Dorcas was alive! Peter stayed for a few days and told many people about Jesus.

Read this exciting story in **Acts chapter 9, verses 40 to 42**.

Dorcas' friends were sad when she died. Cross out the first and second letters, leaving each third letter, to find out how they felt later.

| s | a | h | b | y | a | k | i | p | o | m | p | r | u | y |

Draw Dorcas' friends' faces after she came alive again.

a prayer

Thank you, God, that you can do the most amazing things. Thank you for using Peter to help Dorcas.

People of the new church

Dear SImon,
Thank you for your order for purple cloth. How are the family, and the camel that hurt its foot? I met Paul and his helpers last week. They had come across the sea and then walked all the way here. They have been telling us all about Jesus. It is so exciting. I'm going again tomorrow to hear some more.

Best wishes from Lydia.

Read **Acts chapter 16, verses 12 to 14** to find out where Lydia lived and what her job was. What were Paul, Silas and Timothy doing for God ?

people   telling   Jesus   about

Use the first letter from each picture to find out where you could tell someone about Jesus.

Say thank you for one of your school friends. Talk to God about what they might enjoy doing with you at church

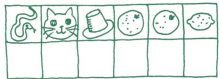

People of the new church

Dear Simon,

Here is the purple cloth you ordered. You will look splendid when it is made up into clothes! Exciting things are happening here. Now I believe in Jesus and so do all the people in my house! We know that Jesus loves us and we are all so happy! Paul and his helpers stayed with me for a few days. All the believers come to my house when we want to pray and praise God! We've learned so much about Jesus from Paul and his friends.

Best wishes from Lydia.

Read this part of Lydia's story in **Acts chapter 16, verse 15**.

Lydia shared her home. Draw toys and food you could share with visitors to your home.

Dear God, help me to be kind and welcoming when anyone comes to my home.

I could share with _____

and _____.

People of the new church

Today we meet Timothy. Read about him in **Acts chapter 16, verses 1 and 2**.

Timothy's mother may have written her diary like this:

"Paul and Silas arrived today to visit the people who love Jesus. Everyone has been telling Paul about Timothy and how he loves God. Paul wants Timothy to go with him and Silas on the rest of his journey. Imagine that – my Timothy travelling to all those faraway places!"

prayer time

People said good things about Timothy. Put a circle round the words they might have said:
Timothy was

kind   horrid

happy   bad-tempered

he loved God

very selfish

Fill in the missing words, then say the prayer.
Dear God, help me to be

[   ] and

[   ] like

Timothy.

Tick the things you would like to be.

People of the new church

Paul knew that God wanted Timothy to do a special job. Timothy was to be Paul's helper, even though he was a young man. Paul showed Timothy how to be a good leader. Timothy travelled about from town to town, sometimes with Paul, sometimes on his own or with others. They visited the Christians and taught them more about Jesus. Timothy had many adventures but whatever happened he always loved and praised God.

Read what Paul wrote to Timothy in **2 Timothy chapter 2, verses 1 and 2**.

God had a special job for Timothy, even while he was quite young. Draw yourself being a helper in a way that would please God.

a prayer

Remember: However old or young you are, you can work for God!

Thank you, God, that whether I am old or young, I can be your special helper. Help me to think hard about the things you would like me to do.

The joke and puzzle page!

Can you work out the names of these people? You have read about all of them in this book.

moTtihy

iMairm

soMes

viDad

diLay

hMaetwt

Drasco

Is your name here?

Why did the chicken lay the table?

She didn't. She laid an egg.

What happens when cats go to buy gloves?

They go for a kitten mitten fittin'.

Fit the words in capital letters into the grid to make another word reading downwards.

It's made up of lots of BOOKS.
It's written by many different PEOPLE.
It's written for EVERYONE.
There are lots of good STORIES in it.
It's the BEST book ever!

What new word have you made?

What does a mouse have for breakfast?

Shredded squeak.

Look out for more
Join in – Jump on!
books
There are 6 altogether.

Great
activity books
for you!

Look out for
hop on and **Let's go…**

If you feel you're
ready to move
on from
Join in – Jump on!
try **Snapshots**. It's
great!

All available from Scripture Union

For more information ring 01908 856006 or contact your national office
www.scriptureunion.org.uk/publishing